Learning Short-take®

SALES FORCE LEADERSHIP

Managing sales teams to high performance

CATHERINE MATTISKE

TPC - The Performance Company Pty Ltd
Level 20, Darling Park
Tower 2, 201 Sussex Street,
Sydney NSW 2000
Australia

ACN 077 455 273
email: tpc@tpc.net.au
Website: www.catherinemattiske.com

© TPC – The Performance Company Pty Limited
First edition published in 2006
Second edition published in 2011
Third edition published in 2022

All rights reserved. Apart from any fair dealing for the purposes of study, research or review, as permitted under Australian copyright law, no part of this publication may be reproduced by any means without the written permission of the copyright owner. Every effort has been made to obtain permission relating to information reproduced in this publication.

The information in this publication is based on the current state of commercial and industry practice, applicable legislation, general law and the general circumstances as at the date of publication. No person shall rely on any of the contents of this publication and the publisher and the author expressly exclude all liability for direct and indirect loss suffered by any person resulting in any way from the use of or reliance on this publication or any part of it. Any options and advice are offered solely in pursuance of the author's and the publisher's intention to provide information, and have not been specifically sought.

For eBook version: By payment of the required fees, you have been granted the non-exclusive, non-transferable right to access and read the text of this e-book on screen. No part of this text may be reproduced, transmitted, downloaded, decompiled, reverse engineered, or stored in or introduced into any information storage retrieval system, in any form or by any means, whether the electronic or mechanical, now known or hereinafter invented, without the express permission of the author.

A catalogue record for this book is available from the National Library of Australia

National Library of Australia
Cataloguing-in-Publication data

Mattiske, Catherine
Sales Force Leadership: Managing Sales Teams to High Performance

ISBN 978-1-921547-21-8

1. Occupational training 2. Learning I. Title

370.113

Distributed by TPC - The Performance Company - www.catherinemattiske.com
For further information contact TPC - The Performance Company, Sydney Australia on +61 (02) 9555 1953.

HELLO.

Welcome to the Learning Short-take® process!

This Learning Short-take® is a bite sized learning package that aims to improve your skills and provide you with an opportunity for personal and professional development to achieve success in your role.

This Learning Short-take® combines self study with workplace activities in a unique learning system to keep you motivated and energized. So let's get started!

Step 1:
What's inside?

- Learning Short-take®. This section contains all of the learning content and will guide you through the learning process.
- Learning Activities. You will be prompted to complete these as you read through.
- Learning Journal. This is a summary of your key learnings. Update it when prompted.
- Skill Development Action Plan. Learning is about taking action. This is your action plan where you'll plan how you will implement your learning.

Step 2:
Complete the Learning Short-take®

- Learning Short-takes® are best completed in a quiet environment that is free of distractions.
- Schedule time in your calendar to complete the Learning Short-take® and prioritize this time as an investment in your own professional development.
- Depending on the title, most participants complete the Learning Short-take® from 90 minutes to 2.5 hours.

Step 3:
Meet with your Manager/Coach

- Schedule a 30 minute meeting with your Manager or Coach.
- At this meeting share your completed Activities, Learning Journal and Skill Development Action Plan.
- Most importantly, discuss and agree on how you will implement your learning in your role.

GET VIP ACCESS
TO YOUR MATERIALS

This Learning Short-take® includes an interactive activity book, associated tools and job aids, plus a bonus eBook.

1 Visit https://www.catherinemattiske.com/books

2 Select your book

3 Click: **VIP ACCESS**

4 Enter the code: **SFL2022353**

WELCOME

Sales Force Leadership
Managing Sales Teams to High Performance

Sales Force Leadership combines self-study with realistic workplace activities to help you develop skills in key facets of sales management. It will guide you in evaluating your current sales management approaches and help you develop new and innovative approaches for application in the workplace.

Sales managers are usually highly competent sales people who are often promoted on their technical skills and selling capability. Apart from product, service and sales knowledge, today's sales manager needs skills in leadership, coaching, counseling, planning, finance, business strategy and innovative ways of dealing with people management issues.

By providing you with new, fresh methods in various facets of sales management, **Sales Force Leadership** will ultimately help you improve the success of your team and reduce the stress of a managing a sales team.

Sales Force Leadership includes the **Sales Meeting Planner, Sales Meeting Plan Summary**, and the **Sales Planning Worksheet**, provided as free downloadable tools.

Now let's get started!

1	**Learning Short-take® > Start here**
2	**Learning Journal** 75
3	**Skill Development Action Plan** 81
4	**Quick Reference** 87
5	**Next Steps** 105

> *"A good leader is a person who takes a little more than his share of the blame and a little less than his share of the credit."*
>
> JOHN C. MAXWELL

"*The best executive is the one who has sense enough to pick good men to do what he wants done, and self-restraint enough to keep from meddling with them while they do it.*"

THEODORE ROOSEVELT

Section 1
LEARNING SHORT-TAKE®

WHAT'S IN THIS LEARNING SHORT-TAKE®

"Success in almost any field depends more on energy and drive than it does on intelligence."

SLOAN WILSON

Table of Contents

How to Complete Your Learning Short-take®	5
Activity Checklist	6
Learning Objectives	7
Let's Get Started	8
Part 1 - The Role of the Sales Manager	9
Part 2 - Sales Planning	17
Part 3 - Organizing the Sales Force	39
Part 4 - Deploying the Sales Team	47
Part 5 - Measuring and Managing Performance	57
Part 6 - Making Sales Meetings Work	67

HOW TO COMPLETE YOUR LEARNING SHORT-TAKE®

1. **Reflect on your skills and abilities** in leading and managing a sales team, and how you use this information to improve effectiveness in your role.

2. **Complete the Initial Skills Self-Assessment.**

3. Highlight specific skill areas that you believe you could develop more. Add these to the **Learning Journal**. Add to your Learning Journal as you go.

4. When you have completed this Learning Short-take® **meet with your Manager/Coach**. In this meeting, you will jointly establish a personal **Skill Development Action Plan**.

5. **Subject to your coach's final review** and assessment, you will either sign off the module, or undertake further skill development as appropriate.

"There is a place in the world for any business that takes care of its customers after the sale."

HARVEY MACKAY

ACTIVITY CHECKLIST

"The best teacher is the one who suggests rather than dogmatizes, and inspires his listener with the wish to teach himself."

EDWARD G. BULWER-LYTTON

During this Learning Short-take® you will be prompted to complete the following activities:

- Activity 1 -   Initial Skills Self-Assessment   12
- Activity 2 -   Think "As is" and "Could be"   15
- Activity 3a - Current Sales Analysis   24
- Activity 3b - Draft Sales Goals   25
- Activity 4a - Finalize Sales Goals   27
- Activity 4b - Communication Plan   28
- Activity 5 -   SWOT Internal Analysis - Strengths & Weaknesses   31
- Activity 6 -   SWOT External Analysis - Opportunities & Threats   32
- Activity 7 -   Create USP for Each Product / Product Line   36
- Activity 8 -   Project Future Sales   37
- Activity 9 -   Sales Team Performance Analysis   55
- Activity 10 - Summarize Sales Plan   56
- Activity 11a - Calculating the Cost of Sales Meetings   70
- Activity 11b - Sales Meeting Planner   71
- Activity 11c - Sales Meeting Plan Summary   72
- Learning Journal   75
- Skill Development Action Plan   81

LEARNING OBJECTIVES

By the end of this Learning Short-take® you be able to:

- Reflect on current sales management skills and identify areas for personal development.
- Compare the current sales environment with possibilities for the future.
- Draft sales goals based on an analysis of current sales.
- Finalize and create a communication strategy for sales goals.
- Analyze the current business using SWOT Analysis.
- Write a unique selling proposition for each product/product line/service.
- Create sales projection for the next financial period.
- Analyze the sales teams current performance including active selling time.
- Establish measures for managing sales team performance.
- Create a plan for upcoming sales meetings to maximize meeting value.
- Create a Skill Development Action Plan.

"The very essence of leadership is that you have to have vision. You can't blow an uncertain trumpet."

THEODORE M. HESBURGH

LET'S GET STARTED

Sales Managers are highly competent sales people who have been promoted on their technical skills and selling capability. Apart from product, service and sales knowledge, today's Sales Manager has skills in leadership, coaching, counseling, planning and business strategy. This is supplemented by a thorough knowledge of budgeting, forecasting and people management issues.

This Learning Short-take® combines self-study with workplace activities to develop skills in key facets of Sales Management. Participants will evaluate their current Sales Management approaches and develop new and innovative approaches for application in their role.

"A sale is not something you pursue, it is something that happens to you while you are immersed in serving your customer."

AUTHOR UNKNOWN

THE ROLE OF THE SALES MANAGER

PART 1

THE ROLE OF THE SALES MANAGER

Competent Sales Managers have the ability to allocate limited time and resources to the activities that meet organizational goals.

Sales leadership is what companies and the sales force expect from a Sales Manager. For an effective Sales Manager, leadership is the key ingredient.

The traditional role of a Sales Manager has changed with the advancement of technology and customers having the ability to purchase from vendors anywhere in the world. The speed of business in the new millennium has also accelerated to the point where new ideas must be implemented quickly to meet the needs of an ever-changing market. Furthermore, sales teams are embracing lifestyle changes that allow them to work on a virtual basis or from home-offices. The result is that Sales Managers today are less involved in the sales process.

To meet these challenges, the effective Sales Manager must juggle many roles. They must understand the changing market, the competition, the general business environment and their suppliers. More importantly they must manage their sales team to deliver organizational goals.

Expectations of Sales Managers

In most cases, organizations expect to see the Sales Manager grow revenue. In addition, some other expectations might be:

- Increased profitability per sale
- Increased sophistication of the organization's sales professionals
- Shortened sales cycles
- Improved forecasting and trend analysis
- Expanded geographic markets
- Deeper or broader market penetration
- Client relationship building
- Expanded brand recognition
- Reduction of perceived sales chaos
- Goals and vision alignment
- Long-range planning for stability
- Market interpretation
- Dealing with problem personnel
- Cross-organization partnering
- Improved competitiveness

"So long as new ideas are created, sales will continue to reach new highs."

DORTHEA BRANDE,
AMERICAN WRITER AND EDITOR

Complete Activity # 1
Initial Skills Self-Assessment

ACTIVITY 1: INITIAL SKILLS SELF-ASSESSMENT

Rate yourself on each of the techniques.
7   is competent and confident, little need for improvement
4   is average, needs improvement
1   is uncomfortable, major need for improvement

- Note specific areas of improvement related to each that you would like to develop. Be sure to include your **reasons** for your rating in each skill.
- As part of starting to think about a personal development plan, identify two or three things you could do to improve your skills in this area and write them in the space provided.

In my role as a Sales Manager, I…	Rating	Reasoning
am a good listener and people have thanked me for listening	1 2 3 4 5 6 7	
look for development opportunities within my sales team and coach regularly	1 2 3 4 5 6 7	
have excellent time management skills and prioritize urgent and important work	1 2 3 4 5 6 7	
effectively get things done through others	1 2 3 4 5 6 7	
consider myself a motivator and have a sense of how motivated each member of my team is	1 2 3 4 5 6 7	
have effective counselling skills and correct behavior without undue stress or emotion	1 2 3 4 5 6 7	
interview and hire new staff effectively	1 2 3 4 5 6 7	
am good at corrective action	1 2 3 4 5 6 7	
consider myself an active mentor to some or all of my sales team	1 2 3 4 5 6 7	
am company-focused - on the organizational goals and the priorities of the business	1 2 3 4 5 6 7	
am a competent trainer and am willing to spend the time necessary to ensure learning for my team	1 2 3 4 5 6 7	

ACTIVITY 1: CONTINUED

In my role as a Sales Manager, I…	Rating	Reasoning
keep my role and the sales effort of the organization in perspective	1 2 3 4 5 6 7	
avoid knee jerk reactions when things go wrong	1 2 3 4 5 6 7	
consider myself a good communicator	1 2 3 4 5 6 7	
am well informed about my organization and industry, and take an active interest in issues that impact my team, or the company.	1 2 3 4 5 6 7	
am consistent in achieving my personal and organizational goals (including making the numbers)	1 2 3 4 5 6 7	
consider myself to have high ethics	1 2 3 4 5 6 7	
actively encourage and have clear development plans for high achieving salespeople on my team	1 2 3 4 5 6 7	
manage my manager effectively	1 2 3 4 5 6 7	
am financially focused	1 2 3 4 5 6 7	
consider the impact of my decisions in relation to other departments in the organization	1 2 3 4 5 6 7	
have good judgment	1 2 3 4 5 6 7	
have, can set, and clearly articulate the sales vision	1 2 3 4 5 6 7	
am very visible within my organization (i.e. people know me)	1 2 3 4 5 6 7	
am good at networking outside my organization in industry related and other social groups	1 2 3 4 5 6 7	

Personal development plan ideas: _____

Now update your Learning Journal (page 75)

© 2022, TPC - The Performance Company Pty Limited. All rights reserved.

Sales Leadership - Big Picture Thinking

A Sales Manager needs to ask the following questions:

- What are the keys to success for my *company* - tomorrow?
- What are the keys to success for my *customers* - tomorrow?
- What are the keys to success for my *salespeople* - tomorrow?

Tomorrow is a metaphor for many time frames - the day after today, next months, six months from now, 12 months from now or whatever timeframe is being considered. Success is ultimately the accumulation of team goals and objectives for a given financial year. By setting objectives and measuring the results against these objectives, there is a higher probability of success.

"Unless you try to do something beyond what you have already mastered, you will never grow."

RONALD E. OSBORN

Complete Activity # 2
Think "As is" & "Could be"

ACTIVITY 2: THINK "AS IS" AND "COULD BE"

Take a Sales Leadership view of the current and potential future state of your organization. Reflect on each of the four Organizational Drivers using the questions to prompt your thoughts.

For a more detailed approach, this tool may be downloaded for your personal use or perhaps to be used at your next Sales Team Meeting as a collaborative team project.

Organizational Driver	Now "As is"	6 months	12 months
Company's Abilities/Capabilities What do they do best? How do they accomplish this today? Why do they do this? Where are they strong as a company (sales team)? What is their current competitive advantage?			
Company's Limits What do they do ineffectively? How do they accomplish this today? Why do they do this? Where are they limited as a company (sales team)? What is their current competitive disadvantage?			

ACTIVITY 2: THINK "AS IS" AND "COULD BE" (CONTINUED)

	Now	6 months	12 months
Company's Value Why do customers buy from your company? What value do they see? What value do they create that your company does not see? What are the alternatives to the value your company is creating?			
Alternatives What alternatives do the customers have? What alternatives will the market create? What will become obsolete? What can radically happen to the budgeted dollars for this product or service?			

Now update your Learning Journal (page 75)

SALES PLANNING

PART 2

SALES PLANNING

Without a plan, there are no definable goals or objectives, no means of evaluating progress, and no ability to measure performance.

A Sales Manager's primary function is to collect sales information, determine the relative value of the data, and then develop and execute a plan to achieve or exceed organizational or corporate goals.

Involving your sales team in the process of planning will provide many benefits, including:

- You will unite your team.
- You will have a common vision. By developing this plan together, everyone will feel ownership of the plan and the direction the company is taking. Do all of your disagreeing in private, and once your team emerges from the planning sessions it will be one team, one plan, one vision.
- You will have woven the flag for the entire company to follow. People follow messages and ideas rather than money and other incentives.
- You will have a well defined company. You will know with clear insight where you've been and, most importantly, where you are going.
- You will know your message and be able to communicate to the rest of the team, your sales reps, your customers and your marketplace.
- You will have a great way to measure your progress. Part of developing a good plan is setting goals and then measuring performance against those goals.
- You will have put in place a successful process that you can use over and over again, year after year.

Make sure that you stick to your plan, but keep it flexible. Try to develop a plan every year. The first year will be the toughest, but the second and third years will be the most dangerous, with the temptation to get lured into the "ditto" mindset. This will happen when you start hearing yourself or your teammates say things like, "We covered that pretty well last year; there is really no reason to cover that again this year."

Treat every year as a new year. Build on the previous year's plan, but please do not dilute the sharpness of your brainstorming this year.

Review Corporate Objectives

Many Sales Managers become so focused on growing sales in their own teams that they lose sight of the broader goals of the organization. In reality, increased sales are often only one component of a larger objective. To stay focused on organizational goals Sales Managers should regularly review corporate activity and watch for indicators of a shift in direction.

Key areas for review:

- Annual reports
- Quarterly reports
- Press releases
- Internal and external speeches by key individuals
- Outside evaluators (financial community and auditors)
- Changes in organizational mission and vision statements
- Your managers
- Your leaders
- Other department heads

"Actually I'm a good sponge. I absorb ideas and put them to use."

THOMAS ALVA EDISON

Sales Goals Fundamentals

Goal Setting Fundamentals

- Anyone who does anything worthwhile has consciously or unknowingly followed through on a goal.
- Goals keep us focused on a purpose.
- They help us through difficult times when many others less motivated would give up.
- A person who wants to get the most out of life often has a number of goals at any given time, in their personal and business lives.

Why are goals important?

- Without them you don't go anywhere!
- Whenever you see anything worthwhile being done anywhere, it is because someone is behind it with a passion, a belief and a goal!
- When it comes to your personal life and your business, goal setting makes the difference between mediocrity and excellence.

Short-term vs Long-term Goals

Short-term goals are defined as those that can be achieved in twelve months or less. Long-term goals are usually defined as those that can be achieved within or beyond 12 months. They tend to be linked with the long-term vision of the organization, must be clearly defined, and must be measurable.

Goal setting explained in 7 easy steps

1. Develop a **DESIRE** to achieve the goal. The desire must be intense. How do you intensify desire? Sit down and write out all the benefits and advantages of achieving your goal. Once the list reaches between 50 and 100 your goal becomes unstoppable.
2. **WRITE** your goal down. Once your goal is written down it becomes substantial and starts etching itself into your subconscious.
3. **IDENTIFY** 1) the obstacles you will need to overcome, 2) the help you will need to acquire, e.g. knowledge, people, organizations. In each case write them out in a clear list and analyze them.
4. **DEADLINE** your goal. Analyze where you are now in relation to the goal and then measure how long you will reasonably need to complete the goal. Then set the latest outside date.
5. Take all the details of steps 3 and 4 and make a **PLAN**. List all the activities and prioritize them. Rewrite the list, optimize it, and perfect it.
6. Get a clear **MENTAL PICTURE** of the goal. Make the mental image crystal clear, vivid in the mind's eye. Play that picture over and over in your mind.
7. Back your plan with **PERSISTENCE** and resolve. Never, never, never give up even when you hit setbacks.

Communicating Goals

Communication skills are critical to the role of Sales Manager. With good communication up and down the line, successful managers drive the goals and objectives of the organization.

Through clear and precise communication, resources can be allocated and managed with less energy and tasks are accomplished with greater speed and accuracy. Good communication also ensures mutual buy-in from all levels.

Sales Goals should be communicated to your boss, your employees, and any other key stakeholders. Communicating goals will help you stay focused, and enable others to assist you in reaching your goals.

Do any of these sound like you?

- "I can't communicate my goals. People will laugh at me and I will look silly."
- "I know what my goals are and I don't need anybody else's help to achieve them."
- "I don't want to record my goals in the event that I don't achieve them, and then look like a failure."

Regularly check progress made toward the goals and be bold enough to refine them where necessary. Then communicate them again and create a support structure to accomplish them. With others helping you, you will achieve more goals than you ever thought possible.

SALES PLANNING WORKSHEET

FREE DOWNLOAD

To download this tool go to
https://www.catherinemattiske.com/books
and follow the online instructions.

Complete Activity # 3a
Current Sales Analysis

Complete Activity # 3b
Draft Sales Goals

ACTIVITY 3A: CURRENT SALES ANALYSIS - EXISTING VS NEW CUSTOMERS

Download the **Sales Planning Worksheet** from https://www.catherinematttiske.com/books

Activity using the Sales Planning Worksheet:

Using the Sales Planning Worksheet, complete Section 1:

- **Current Sales Analysis** - For each current product line or market segment, fill in the dollar amounts (or your currency) and percentages for the current year's sales

You will complete the remaining parts of the Sales Planning Worksheet later.

Now update your Learning Journal (page 75)

ACTIVITY 3B: DRAFT SALES GOALS

 Continue in your downloaded **Sales Planning Worksheet** from
https://www.catherinematttiske.com/books

Activity using the Sales Planning Worksheet:

Using the Sales Planning Worksheet, complete Section 2:

- **Sales Goals** - Using the guidelines from the reference manual, draft sales goals for your business. Focus on three areas: goals for the organization, customers and your sales team.

You will complete the remaining parts of the Sales Planning Worksheet later.

Activity Prompt:
Sales Manager Expectations
- Increased profitability per sale
- Increased sophistication of the organization's sales professionals
- Shortened sales cycles
- Improved forecasting and trend analysis
- Expanded geographic markets
- Deeper or broader market penetration
- Client relationship building
- Expanded brand recognition
- Reduction of perceived sales chaos
- Goals and vision alignment
- Long-range planning for stability
- Market interpretation
- Dealing with problem personnel
- Cross-organization partnering
- Improved competitiveness

Now update your Learning Journal (page 75)

"Nothing can stop the person with the right mental attitude from achieving his goal; nothing on earth can help the person with the wrong mental attitude."

W.W. ZIEGE

Complete Activity # 4a
Finalize Sales Goals

Complete Activity # 4b
Communication Plan

ACTIVITY 4A: FINALIZE SALES GOALS

 Continue in your downloaded **Sales Planning Worksheet** from
https://www.catherinematttiske.com/books

Activity using the Sales Planning Worksheet:

Using the Sales Planning Worksheet, complete Section 3:

- **Finalize Sales Goals** - In this Activity you will refine your sales goals that you drafted earlier. Before you can approach customers or your sales team and meet your sales goals, you need to fully understand and be committed to your direction. Answer the questions to better understand your direction in terms of market segmentation, customer mix and product mix. Then, finalize your sales goals.

You will complete the remaining parts of the Sales Planning Worksheet later.

Now update your Learning Journal (page 75)

ACTIVITY 4B: COMMUNICATION PLAN

Create a plan of how and to whom you will communicate your sales goals.

Now update your Learning Journal (page 75)

Business Analysis - SWOT

Perhaps the simplest and most effective tool for analyzing the business is S.W.O.T. - Strengths, Weaknesses, Opportunities, and Threats. This approach provides an opportunity to think through business realities on which you build your plans. As the organization is changing, so are the customers, competitors, suppliers, and the general market environment.

Strengths and Weaknesses focus on the internal organization while Opportunities and Threats focus on the external environment. A SWOT Analysis can be developed on a business in general or on six specific focus areas of the business that can be implemented and managed:

1. **Product** (what are we selling?)
2. **Process** (how are we selling it?)
3. **Customer** (to whom are we selling it?)
4. **Distribution** (how does it reach them?)
5. **Finance** (what are the prices, costs and investments?)
6. **Administration** (and how do we manage all this?)

SWOT assists Sales Managers to understand and evaluate what is good and bad about a business in general or a particular proposition. Overall the aim is improvement, so using a SWOT analysis the Sales Manager works on identifying the actual and potential opportunities (prioritize and optimize). Then uses the organizations strengths (maintain, build and leverage) to capitalize on each opportunity, whilst working on ways to mitigate weakness (remedy or exit) and potential threats (address and counter).

SWOT Example

Strengths
- Product portfolio
- Cash reserves
- Management team
- Stable, long-term reputation
- Strong brand identity
- Defined market position perception

Weaknesses
- Aging customer base
- Old technology
- Fragmented distribution network
- Perceived poor customer service
- Decreasing margins
- Global infrastructure

Opportunities
- Diversified product line
- New acquisitions
- Newer, younger markets
- International markets
- Pull-through sales by customer service

Threats
- Market elimination
- Competition with newer technology
- Zero margins due to too many competitors
- International competitors with low labor costs

Complete Activity # 5
SWOT Internal Analysis - Strengths & Weaknesses

Complete Activity # 6
SWOT External Analysis - Opportunities & Threats

ACTIVITY 5: SWOT INTERNAL ANALYSIS - STRENGTHS & WEAKNESSES

Continue in your downloaded **Sales Planning Worksheet** from
https://www.catherinematttiske.com/books

Activity using the Sales Planning Worksheet:

Using the Sales Planning Worksheet, complete Section 4:

- **SWOT Analysis – Strengths & Weaknesses** - Consider your Organizational/Departmental Strengths & Weaknesses.

You will complete the remaining parts of the Sales Planning Worksheet later.

Now update your Learning Journal (page 75)

ACTIVITY 6: SWOT EXTERNAL ANALYSIS - OPPORTUNITIES & THREATS

 Continue in your downloaded **Sales Planning Worksheet** from https://www.catherinematttiske.com/books

 **Activity using the Sales Planning Worksheet:**

Using the Sales Planning Worksheet, complete Section 4:

- **SWOT Analysis – Opportunities & Threats** - What are the opportunities and threats that currently face your business?

You will complete the remaining parts of the Sales Planning Worksheet later.

Now update your Learning Journal (page 75)

The Unique Selling Proposition

What differentiates your product(s) from the competition? Why is it better? What is better? What is your competitive advantage? This is your USP, **the Unique Selling Proposition.**

Your "USP" is a concise statement which describes unique features that distinguish your product(s) or service(s) from your competitors, and provides customers the opportunity to justify their purchase decision.

The USP answers an important question for the customer "What can your product or service do for me that nobody else can?" Your USP should be crafted to answer this question.

"The majority of people meet with failure because of their lack of persistence in creating new sale management plans to take the place of those which fail."

NAPOLEON HILL

Crafting Your USP

The process of creating your USP is not a simple task. However the more generic your business, the greater the importance of developing a USP, and the greater the return on the time invested. Generally a business has more than one USP - one for the overall business and others specific to market segments.

The process of creating your USP begins by answering four questions about your business and product:

- What is unique about your business or product when compared to the competition ("Unique Characteristics")?
- Of your Unique Characteristics, which are most important to your community or market?
- Which of your Unique Characteristics are not easily imitated by the competition?
- Which of your Unique Characteristics can be easily communicated and understood by your customers to be?

Without a USP most businesses leave their success to chance. Never forget that it is your pursuit of uniqueness, not excellence that will set you apart from the crowd. The deciding factor will be the customer's perception that you offer something different, something not available from the competition.

A lower price is not sufficient as your USP. Think of other issues which are important to the customer such as packaging, quality, color, availability (distribution and merchandising), service, etc. The whole package of products or services offered.

Niche Marketing

To develop a niche, you should be looking for anomalies in the market. In marketing terms an anomaly is an unmet need that needs to be satisfied. To support a profitable business, the need must be relatively widespread or growing rapidly.

The Simpler, the Better

The best USPs are those that are easily remembered. If people can't find or remember your message then your effort is for nothing. Remember that customers are not willing to spend any more time then necessary to read your message. As such, successful messages are short, easily understood, and leave no room for confusion.

The final test of your USP is to read it to someone not related to your business. Ask the listener to restate your message in his or her own words. If what you hear is accurate, you have created a usable USP. If the listener cannot restate your message accurately, start over again. Don't test it on someone who knows you and your business, and never ask if they understood your message, most people will just nod yes to this question. Your future hinges on the ability to communicate the uniqueness of your business. So take every step necessary to ensure accurate feedback when testing your USP.

Complete Activity # 7
Create a USP for Each Product / Product Line

Complete Activity # 8
Project Future Sales

ACTIVITY 7: CREATE A USP FOR EACH PRODUCT / PRODUCT LINE

Continue in your downloaded **Sales Planning Worksheet** from https://www.catherinematttiske.com/books

Activity using the Sales Planning Worksheet:

Using the Sales Planning Worksheet, complete Section 5:

- **Product / Product Line USP (Unique Selling Proposition)** - Create a Unique Selling Proposition for products or services that are sold/delivered to your customer.

You will complete the remaining parts of the Sales Planning Worksheet later.

Now update your Learning Journal (page 75)

ACTIVITY 8: PROJECT FUTURE SALES

Continue in your downloaded **Sales Planning Worksheet** from
https://www.catherinematttiske.com/books

Activity using the Sales Planning Worksheet:

Using the Sales Planning Worksheet, complete Section 6:

- **Project Future Sales** - Through research and/or discussions, find out where next year's sales are expected to come from in various market segments. These may be listed by individual product / product line / service (as per your list from the previous activity.

You will complete the remaining parts of the Sales Planning Worksheet later.

Now update your Learning Journal (page 75)

"

*"The leaders who work most effectively,
it seems to me, never say 'I'. And that's not because
they have trained themselves not to say 'I'. They
don't think 'I'. They think 'we'; they think 'team'.
They understand their job to be to make the team
function. They accept responsibility and don't
sidestep it, but 'we' gets the credit. This is what
creates trust, what enables you to get the task done."*

PETER DRUCKER

"

ORGANIZING THE SALES FORCE

PART 3

ORGANIZING THE SALES FORCE

Finding and Recruiting the Best Sales Team

Salesperson Competencies

Sales Managers want salespeople to have a high degree of quality and competence in the tasks they do. Here is a sample list of sales competencies:

- Selling skills
- Sales focused
- Presentation skills
- Professionalism
- Sales cycle control
- Customer knowledge
- Negotiating skills
- Ability to get things done
- Qualifying skills
- Customer relationship
- Personal confidence
- Prospecting skills

The list could be endless. Sales Managers need to develop their own list of skills, traits, work habits, etc, that their salespeople are required to have.

> **For more information** on Recruiting Sales Professionals refer to the Learning Short-take® "Recruiting for Results". Available from catherinemattiske.com website.

Hiring New Salespeople - The Job Description

The job description is something that must be prepared before the interview process begins. It describes the tasks and duties that need to be completed and should include:

- Basic requirements of the job
- Tasks required to be completed
    - Sales call requirements
    - Reporting responsibilities
    - Expense responsibilities
    - Time allocation
    - Management expectations
- Position particulars
    - Territory
    - Customers
    - Quota and revenue expectations
- First 90-day goals and objectives
- First-year objectives

Preparing to Interview - Reading Resumes

One amusing description of a resume is the following:

"Resumes are like mirrors in a funhouse. They offer a distorted image of reality… to deceive the eye".

A resume is an objective document if it is read correctly. Sales Managers get a picture of the person, although it is the picture that the applicant wants you to have! You need to read each word and evaluate the nonverbal messages as well.

The Interview Process

There are essentially five characteristics of great salespeople.

Natural Curiosity

Successful salespeople have a natural curiosity. They always want to know 'why'. They take this inquisitiveness 'why'. They take this inquisitiveness into the market and really know how to probe and ask good questions. They also tend to have good listening skills, which helps them ask great questions. Great salespeople do not always have the answers, but they always have great questions.

Complex to Simple

Successful salespeople can make the most complicated issue seem simple. At least they can explain it in simple terms. A great salesperson would not make the following statement:

"The complexity of this new product is evolving from our UL-IV to our UL-V program. It also comes with built-in Wifi, 4G/5G and our new ADT modules with integrated interface, all designed to run at even greater gigahertz speeds."

The salesperson who made this claim knew exactly what they were talking about. The problem is they were the only one in the room who understood it. Great salespeople avoid making themselves look good by impressing the buyer with their product knowledge. They communicate in simplistic terms and are understood because of it.

For example, the sales person could have said the following instead:

"The advancement we now have in our new product will help you do the job twice as fast. Along with our additional modules, you will even be able to accomplish the task at least ten times faster."

Great salespeople know they are great. They have a quiet competence about themselves. They do not need a "job". They are "A" players. They can get a "job" anywhere. During the interview, they are evaluating the Sales Manager and the company and want to find out as much as they can. Second, they know it makes the interviewer feel good to have them talk about themselves. It is true on a sales call, so it obviously works in an interview.

Ability to Flip

As discussed earlier, the ability to flip is an important one. Getting the buyer to talk is a characteristic of a successful salesperson. The person who flips in an interview has control of the interview or sales call.

All Perspectives

The successful salesperson can see things from all perspectives. The great salespeople can hold a conversation from different viewpoints when the situation calls for it. Watch for the candidate to switch from "I" to "You" to "They" mode when the situation calls for it.

The Golden Rule of Hiring

It is easier to teach a competent salesperson what to sell than to teach a product-competent person how to sell.

Now update your Learning Journal (page 75)

Manage the Sales Team

Distribution curve of salespeople

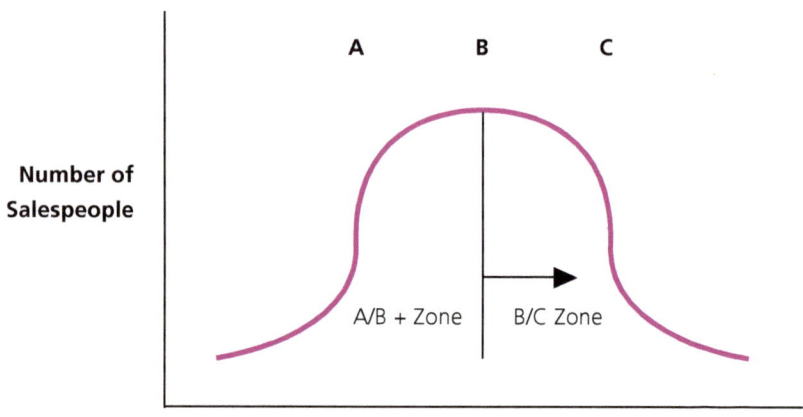

When looking at a sales team, the chart shows a typical distribution of salespeople, ranged as A, B, and C players. There are approximately 20-25% A or top performers, about 50% B or middle of the road performers, and the rest, about 25%, C or low performers. Your sales organization may resemble this bell curve.

The question to be asked is: How much time is being spent on B and C players? In other words, what percentage of voice mails, e-mails, requests for sales calls, salespeople hanging out in the office, assistance to save a sales situation, or excuses about slips in the forecast are from the B and C players? Probably too many.

The Sales Manager 80/20 Rule

In a reactive world, Sales Managers spend much of their time doing what they can to help their team achieve a target. They work the deals and situations that are presented to them; they fill their calendar with appointments booked by their salespeople, and help to finalize negotiations. When all of this is done, they believe they have helped the sales process along. However, this is a reactive approach to sales management and the people who request the largest amount of time and assistance are generally not the people the sales manager should be spending time with.

Sales Managers should aim to spend 80% of their time with A players, coaching them to become A+ players.

- 'A' players need to drive the sales culture and are where the largest return for effort is. They rarely seek advice.
- 'C' players, when given assistance, will always come back and ask for more, which often means the same requests over and over.
- If you do not spend time with the 'A' players, they will most likely resign or move to another part of the organization.

Focus on the top performers. It makes monetary sense, it drives the culture, it sends a clear message to the sales team and to the rest of the company. It is also more rewarding for the sales team and the Sales Manager.

Raising the Bar for Existing Sales Team Members

As performance standards plateau in the sales team, you must continue drive a higher and higher levels of performance. Measure where each team member is, where you want them to be, how much time is available to improve their performance, and what their rate of learning is. Also, develop a performance improvement plan that is based on where you want them to be both in the short term and in the longer term.

Active Selling Time

Consider the following calculation as to why it's important to recruit A players:

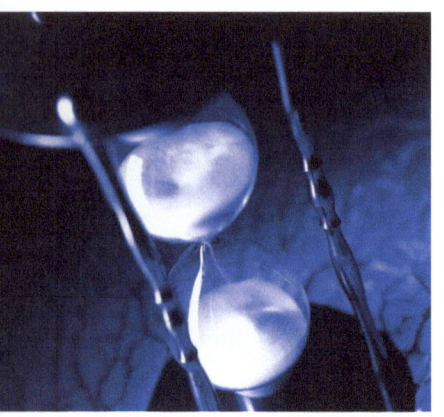

Total number of days in a year	365
Less:	
Weekends	104
Annual Holidays	20
Public Holidays	11
Illness	5
Training/Conferences	10
Other	5
NET AVAILABLE DAYS	**210**

Total number of hours in a year (210 days at 10hrs/day)		2100
Less (Time Stealers):	Day	Year
Travelling/Driving	3.5	735
Waiting	0.75	157
Admin/Meetings	1.5	315
Lunch	0.5	105
Personal	0.25	52
TOTAL TIME STEALERS (hours)		**1364**

Total Time	2,100 hours
Less Time Stealers	1,364 hours
Net Available	736 hours
Per Month	66 hours
Per Week	15 hours
Per Day	**3 hours**

3 hours per day for what?

DEPLOYING THE SALES TEAM

PART 4

DEPLOYING THE SALES TEAM

"If eighty percent of your sales come from twenty percent of all of your items, just carry those twenty percent."

HENRY KISSINGER

There are three approaches to strategically deploying the sales team. Sales Managers can organize a sales team by:

1. Geographic assignments
2. Account assignments
3. Product assignments

Geographic Assignments

Many sales organizations divide up a territory by state, region, county, zip codes, or however it best makes sense at the time. Geographic organization is usually the easiest and cleanest way to divide a sales territory.

Account Assignments

Dividing up a territory by named accounts or by named industries is also a clean way to manage a sales team when there are large accounts that need coordination across territories.

Product Assignments

Organizing by product means letting certain salespeople focus on selling particular products. This is a good way to manage sales territories when product specialization is necessary, and the salesperson is required to provide product value add. Product specialization is also a way many companies push low-end products to gain market penetration.

Types of Sales Territories

Type of Sales Territory	Advantages	Disadvantages
Geographic	<ul><li>Easy, Clean, and Minimal Disputes</li><li>Less Travel Cost</li><li>Deeper Geographical Penetration</li></ul>	<ul><li>Less Specialization</li><li>Less Customer Continuity</li><li>Constant Change with Growth</li></ul>
Account	<ul><li>High Customer Centric</li><li>Deep Industry Penetration</li><li>High in Relationship Selling</li><li>Maximizes 80/20 Rule</li></ul>	<ul><li>Higher Travel Budgets</li><li>Less Geographic Coverage</li><li>Low New Account Focus</li></ul>
Product	<ul><li>High Value-Add Sale Approach</li><li>Adaptable to Fast-Changing Products</li><li>Market Penetration</li></ul>	<ul><li>Less Relationship Selling</li><li>Less Customer Focus</li><li>Can Get Complex</li></ul>

"There's a way to do it better, find it."

THOMAS EDISON

The Proactive Sales Matrix

The Proactive Sales Matrix is a way for the Sales Manager and the salesperson mutually to define where to prioritize the salesperson's most precious resource - time. The matrix adds a new dimension to the sales forecast. Typically, a salesperson forecasts the current opportunities in an A, B, C type of forecast.

- **A - The current hot prospects**. These accounts are what the salesperson is banking on. 90% likelihood is typically assigned to these prospects.

- **B - The medium prospects**. Typically, these accounts are somewhere in the pipeline and are considered work in process. 60-70% likelihood is usually assigned to these prospects.

- **C - The lukewarm prospects**. More than likely, these are the prospects just being qualified - the prospects that are just starting in the sales cycle. 20-40% likelihood is usually used for these accounts.

The table below shows a typical A, B, C type of sales forecast.

The Reactive Sales Forecast

	Forecast	Factor	Total
A Prospects			
Smith Co	$100,000	90%	$90,000
Jones Corp	75,000	90%	67,500
Davidson, Inc	45,000	90%	40,500
B Prospects			
Johnson Corp	$125,000	60%	$75,000
Great Co	50,000	60%	30,000
Glass Inc	55,000	60%	33,000
The A Co	125,000	60%	75,000
ASSCO	200,000	60%	120,000
C Prospects			
Oniete Inc	$500,000	20%	$100,000
Land One	110,000	20%	22,000
SDDTR	75,000	20%	15,000
Bocast Corp	35,000	20%	7,000
Beckett Intl	45,000	20%	9,000
Wills Co	30,000	20%	6,000
		Forecast	$690,000
		Quarter Quota	$650,000
		% for Quarter	106.15%

This is reactive sales planning. From the Sales Manager's perspective there are some flaws in the type of reporting shown above:

- Medium and lukewarm prospects are included in the forecast.
- This forecast shows what the salesperson has done, and not what can be done.
- It reports what activities have brought accounts up to their current status and then guesses the probability of future activity and potential.
- In a typical forecast like this, 80-90% of the probability is based on what sales activities have been done in the past, and about 10-20% of the probability is based on what the future activity is. These percentages need to be reversed.
- What is missing from this typical forecast is future activities.

The Sales Matrix allows the manager to effectively communicate to the sales team what is needed and what is important. It does this by adding a second dimension to the A, B, C forecast method, a second digit. By adding a second digit to the matrix, there is an AA prospect instead of an A prospect. The first digit stands for current or past activity of the account, and the second digit signifies future activity of the account. Additionally, the letter itself signifies the dollar amount (or other measurable unit) that is being evaluated (see table below).

The letters must represent dollar figures. Use whatever dollar amounts make sense for your sales environment. For example:

A = Sales greater than $100,000
B = Sales between $30,000 and $100,000
C = Sales less than $30,000

The Proactive Sales Matrix

The Proactive Sales Matrix allows the manager to assist the salespeople to plan how to spend their time and resource. It gives the salespeople an objective view of what they are doing and what they need to do to be successful in the future, not just focusing on what they have done in the past. It also gives the manager an objective communications tool to discuss frequencies and competencies with the sales team.

Old Method of Forecasting

A
B
C

Revised Method of Forecasting

Example: Customer has spent over $100,000 in the past		
Example: Customer likely to spend over $100,000 in the next 90-120 days		

AA	AB	AC
BA	BB	BC
CA	CB	CC

- Example - Basing the forecast on a sales window of 90-120 days an AA account is one that has spent over $100,000 in the past and that has the potential in the next 90 to 120 days to spend over $100,000.

- Example - CA prospect status represents that the account currently or in the past has spent less than $30,000 and has the potential in 90 to 120 days to spend more than $100,000.

Alternatively, another option for the matrix is to designate the second digit to represent future time. The first digit signifies today. For the second digit the following time spans have been assumed: A - within 90 days, B - 90 to 180 days, C - >180 days. The Sales Manager should decide on the way the sales matrix will work and implement it to the sales team.

Completed Sales Matrix - 3 Zones: Active, Maintain & Dead

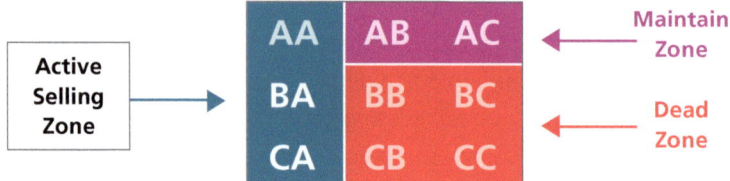

Maintain Zone

The Maintain Zone, also called the Comfort Zone, contains customers who are important to the business. They have spent a lot of money in the past, however, at the current time, your company should not spend a whole lot of time here. The customers current budget or buying window does not require a lot of time. Why do salespeople spend time here? Because these people are their friends and they feel comfortable in calling on them, seeing them again, or just hanging out with them. There is no short-term financial gain, but it is better than having to prospect for new business.

Active Selling Zone

The Active Selling Zone contains prospects that have the potential to spend a lot of money with the company in a short period of time, and time should be invested in this zone. This is the case especially in the BA and CA zones, because these are accounts that have a large enough potential to justify spending precious time with, like on a new major deal that the competition is going to lose.

Complete Activity # 9
Sales Team Performance Analysis

ACTIVITY 9: SALES TEAM PERFORMANCE ANALYSIS

 Continue in your downloaded **Sales Planning Worksheet** from https://www.catherinematttiske.com/books

Activity using the Sales Planning Worksheet:

Using the Sales Planning Worksheet, complete Section 7:

- **Sales Team Performance Analysis** - Create a plan for analyzing the effectiveness and efficiencies of the sales team. The prompting questions will assist.

You will complete the remaining parts of the Sales Planning Worksheet later.

Now update your Learning Journal (page 75)

Complete Activity # 10
Summarize Sales Plan

ACTIVITY 10: SUMMARIZE SALES PLAN

 Continue in your downloaded **Sales Planning Worksheet** from https://www.catherinematttiske.com/books

Activity using the Sales Planning Worksheet:

Using the Sales Planning Worksheet, complete Section 8:

- **Summarize Plan** - Summarize your Sales Plan into key action points.

Congratulations! You have now completed your plan.

Now update your Learning Journal (page 75)

MEASURING AND MANAGING PERFORMANCE

"Even if you're on the right track, you'll get run over if you just sit there."

WILL ROGERS

The ability to accurately predict changes in revenue, margins, expenses, competitive actions, market needs and wants, and the potential of the sales team is the key to sales success.

Revenue Results

Revenue results are a good measure of past performance and therefore can be a good indicator or long term future performance. However, when used to measure performance in the short term, revenue is less useful. Often the measurement comes too late: the market has changed too fast, territories have been realigned, or management has been reorganized.

Focusing on revenue does not measure the tasks and functions that build up the revenue. There really is little that can be done to affect revenue. It is more important to measure what can be done to affect the functions that make up revenue.

Other Measurements - Frequency

Sales Managers want to keep their people busy. To ensure that 'busy' is actually productive, they need to be specific about what they want their salespeople to do. Here is a sample list of frequency metrics:

- Sales calls per week
- Weekly prospecting
- Home office visits
- Reports on time

- Sales proposals per week
- Executive sales calls
- Sales funnel quantity
- Sales calls on key accounts

- Executive visits
- Demonstrations
- Focus on A prospects
- Time Management

Make a list of the frequencies you need from your salespeople over the next 90 to 180 days. Whatever they are, establish them as objectives and measure them.

Later in this Learning Short-take® we will discuss Managing Time - specifically, Managing Active Selling Time.

"Success seems to be connected with action. Successful people keep moving. They make mistakes, but they don't quit."

CONRAD HILTON

Watching for Negative Results

Always be aware of the actual behaviors resulting from the sales team. Clues that something is wrong with a sales person could include:

- Declining sales revenue
- Decreasing gross margins
- Lack of broad product portfolio sales
- New product failure rate
- Concentration on limited number of customers
- Poor customer-satisfaction surveys
- Competitor gains
- Long sales cycles
- Inordinate number of failed opportunities
- Negative external perception of the sales professional
- Resistance to change
- Risk avoidance
- Cross-organizational communications breakdown
- Secretiveness, lack of information sharing, and no teaming
- Anger, frustration and conflict

Coaching vs Counselling

Sales Managers coach from their own experience, or from what they "know to be so" based on logic. Coaching is a series of steps or activities designed to improve the performance of a salesperson.

Coaching sales calls involve the Sales Manager going out with a salesperson and assisting that person based on observations of the call itself, or based on what the Sales Manager has learned from previous experience.

Counselling comes from the emotional side. Counselling is very personal and very empathetic. It is a process to use when the Sales Manager wants to elicit responses from the salesperson and arrive at a mutual arrangement. Counselling is a series of steps or activities designed to correct a specific problem affecting a salesperson or other employee.

"Leaders don't create followers, they create more leaders."

TOM PETERS

"Don't tell people how to do things, tell them what to do and let them surprise you with their results."

GEORGE S. PATTON

Accompanying Salespeople on Sales Visits

There are two types of sales calls on which a Sales Manager may accompany the salesperson. It's important to identify which one is the correct choice for which opportunity. The sales call objective should be stated before the call itself. A successful sales call is planned ahead of the call, and the outcome is discussed.

1. **The coaching call.** The salesperson has complete control. The value of the call should be low to allow for mistakes and the creation of a learning environment where the Sales Manager does not feel compelled to jump in. Any problems can then be discussed after the call is over.

2. **The joint sales call.** The Sales Manager has an active role in the call. When a sales situation is at a critical phase, or the salesperson is new, or another reason where the call needs management expertise. The joint sales call is one where both parties plan to add value to the call, not to take over each other's role.

Reward and Recognition

Rewards are a planned device you use to tell the sales team formally that they are doing something right. Rewards should be based on their having accomplished something that the manager wanted them to do, and they should not be just revenue based.

- A reward for making the most sales calls in person to vice presidents and above in a thirty-day time period.
- A reward for the most list-price deals in a sixty-day period.
- A weekly award for the best win-win negotiation session.
- Monthly merit badge or similar token-award ceremonies, with letterman jackets, sweaters, or plaques. Monthly awards for the most qualified prospects in the A sales funnel.
- The Magic Wand Award for the best deal of the week.
- Weekly notes on individual sales team stationery.
- Monthly stack-ranking charts to identify who is leading and trailing the pack.

"Sales are contingent upon the attitude of the salesman - not the attitude of the prospect."
W. CLEMENT STONE'
AMERICAN BEST SELLING AUTHOR

Professional Development Opportunities

Top salespeople want to learn and grow. For some, it is the # 1 motivational factor. The top salespeople should be kept focused on bringing in revenue and adding value, but there is also a need to come up with some creative ideas that will help them to push themselves and the rest of the sales team. Here are some pointers:

- Have the top salespeople come up with some additional ideas.

- The Sales Manager and salespeople should discuss and agree on a professional development plan in addition to their current quota plan. Top performers know they need to achieve their target as well as carry out added responsibilities. They will find a way to do both.

- Training is a very effective tool. Top salespeople and top Sales Managers want management to invest in their careers. Training is a win-win for the employee and the employer.

Positive motivations centred around praise, rewards, and professional development challenges are a key element in hiring, motivating, and keeping top performers. They are a major part of sales team culture.

Compensation Programs

In order to attract, recruit, retain, and develop the very best people for your sales team, you have to establish a clear reward system that is logically linked to the overall objectives of the organization.

The challenges involved in developing a successful compensation plan are many. For one thing, money is not the only form of reward desired by individuals. Their personal and professional goals, along with the necessity of meeting or exceeding corporate-directed goals, must be taken into consideration. Some additional forms of compensation may include bonuses, benefits, increased authority or responsibility, increased visibility, increased autonomy and independence, reimbursed expenses, or other personal wants and needs. This balance depends on several factors, including:

"The object of a salesperson is not to make sales, but to make customers."

- The needs of the company
- The needs of the salesperson
- The level of salesperson you want to attract
- The salesperson's ability to influence the sale
- The type of product or services sold
- The specific behaviors or competencies necessary for success

The Sales Leader Role in Compensation

As the link between senior management and the sales team's activities in the target market, it is your responsibility to ensure that the total compensation plan is always in line with a continuously changing business environment.

1. Direct Compensation. Salary or fixed pay, performance or at-risk commission, deferred bonuses.

2. Benefits. Social security, health or other insurance, profit sharing, stock options, tuition reimbursement, etc.

"Obstacles are those frightful things you see when you take your eyes off your goal."

HENRY FORD

3. Reimbursed expenses. Travel expenses or car allowance, entertainment, communications, office or technology expenses, etc.

Now update your Learning Journal (page 75)

MAKING SALES MEETINGS WORK

PART 6

MAKING SALES MEETINGS WORK

Communication is a key part of any sales team's success. How often and how well a sales team communicates externally to its customers and internally to its members goes a long way to establishing a winning culture and long-term success.

Reactive Sales Meeting Focus	Proactive Sales Meeting Focus
1. Product knowledge	1. Selling skills
2. Company speakers	2. Communication / presentation skills
3. Team building	3. Product knowledge
4. Free time	4. Teambuilding
5. Communication skills	5. Company speakers

Reasons to Hold a Sales Meeting

1) Train or retrain

a) Ongoing training should be consistent with the overall sales philosophy.

2) Improve communications

a) One way to keep the lines of communication open is to be sure your people hear about policy changes *from you*. When there is good or bad news to share, tell everyone at once in a sales meeting.

3) Motivate the team

a) Keeping the team's morale high is one of those leadership skills that comes with the job. Your people should always leave the sales meeting better than when they arrived/joined.

b) One part of motivation is recognition. Use sales meetings as a time to give recognition to top performers and to people who are improving.

4) Solve problems

a) You are also a trouble-shooter. A meeting can be devoted to problems, but make sure they are relevant to everyone and well controlled.

5) Introduce new products or contests

a) Get everyone motivated and ready to go.

b) The importance of a new product or sales contest can be dramatically enhanced with the announcement coming from a Senior Leader or expert in that area.

Complete Activity # 11a
Calculating the Cost of Sales Meetings

Complete Activity # 11b
Sales Meeting Planner

Complete Activity # 11c
Sales Meeting Plan Summary

ACTIVITY 11A: CALCULATING THE COST OF SALES MEETINGS

Calculate Sales Meeting Cost

	Sample	Calculate your team
Average salary per annum	$80,000	
Average hourly salary (annual salary divided by 48 weeks* divided by 25 hours per week) (25 hours of true sales work per week)	$66	
Multiplied by number of people	Say 5 in the team $330 per hour	
Sales Meeting duration (2 hours) = 10 people hours	$660 for 2 hour meeting + opportunity cost of having 10 hours of lost sales productivity + travel time + preparation time	
	What is the true cost of your sales meetings?	

*52 weeks minus the average number of vacation weeks

Now update your Learning Journal (page 75)

ACTIVITY 11B: SALES MEETING PLANNER

 Download the **Sales Meeting Planner** from https://www.catherinematttiske.com/books

 **Activity using the Sales Meeting Planner:**

Plan a series of meetings using the Sales Meeting Planner.

Now update your Learning Journal (page 75)

ACTIVITY 11C: SALES MEETING PLAN SUMMARY

Download the **Sales Meeting Plan Summary** from https://www.catherinematttiske.com/books

Activity using the Sales Meeting Plan Summary:

Using the Sales Meeting Plan Summary, consolidate your thoughts to create a plan for the next three sales meetings.

Now update your Learning Journal (page 75)

ANNUAL SALES MEETING PLANNER

Annual Sales Meeting Checklist

1. **Choose the best location:** Choose an environment for relaxed fun and learning, such as a resort with sporting options and nice meeting rooms. Make your venue fit your meeting. If you bring your team to an exotic place as a reward for great efforts, you will probably provoke an uprising if you try to keep them in meetings all day. If you are there to work on your plan, work them in a concentrated way from seven in the morning until 12 noon or 1pm and then allow them to leave and enjoy the rest of their day. This works less well at places where late night entertainment is offered (e.g. Las Vegas etc), where many of your group may be bleary eyed early in the morning. If it is really to be a working meeting where you need focused time all day choose a hotel in a non-destination city, or close to home, where temptations and competition for attention are fewer.

2. **Ask for areas for development:** Ask the participants about problems and needs, strengths and frustrations, themselves and their goals. Use questionnaires to personalize the training portion of the meeting.

3. **Spend Lavishly On Trophies, Plaques and Certificates:** Napoleon noted "a man would give his life for a simple bit of colored ribbon." Money spent on recognition is some of the best money you'll ever spend. Recognition, no matter how small, motivates your sales force to take action. Base awards on activities that anyone can do and win. Better to give lots of plaques to lots of people. Create several categories to involve lots of winners: biggest sale, most new customers, highest volume, fewest lost customers, most improved, fewest returns or cancellations. If you give away a trip to a luxury resort for the top salesperson, everyone knows who will win as soon as the contest is announced and those who haven't won lose motivation.

4. **Hire a Good Photographer:** Capture candid shots throughout the meeting. Show them randomly on a huge screen during the closing festivities to stimulate conversation, reminiscences and bonding. Use them after the meeting in company publications to remind the attendees of the good times and to inspire the folks who didn't attend to catch the next one.

5. **Start With A Bang:** Do group fun first. Play a round of golf, have a big dinner the evening before, or a motivational speaker.

6. **Play Upbeat Music Before, After and During Breaks:** People subconsciously know its break time and mentally shift gears. When the music goes off, people drift back to their seats and slip back into business mode. Choose instrumentals over vocals; the goal is to set a mood, rather than entertain.

7. **Provide an Executive Welcome:** Have a short and sweet welcome-about 10 minutes - from the Chief Executive Officer at the first formal gathering. This could include a personal story and thanks for the group's hard work.

8. **Review The Wins:** List the victories of the past year and repeat a few (short) stories of the biggest triumphs.

9. **Spotlight One Or Two People:** Have them tell the group how they made a big sale, saved a deal or used a new technique.

10. **Thank The Team:** Thank-and applaud-the people that made it happen.

11. **Award The Best:** Let the CEO and sales manager present high-quality plaques, trophies and prizes. Have several categories to involve lots of winners.

12. **Plan Together:** The next year is the focus of the meeting. Let the sales team be part of the plan. Don't just give them the next year's game plan. Let the sales team help make it. Making your sales team take ownership of sales goals is only possible when they participate in the process.

Section 2
LEARNING JOURNAL

The Learning Journal is used throughout the process to record your key learnings, hot tips and things to remember.

Update your Learning Journal at anytime. Ensure you complete your Learning Journal after you finish each activity. Then turn back to the Learning Short-take® to continue your learning.

LEARNING JOURNAL

As you work through this Learning Short-take®, make detailed notes on this page of the lessons you have learned and any useful skill areas. For each lesson or refresher point think about how you could further develop this skill. Your coach will want to discuss these with you in your Skill Development Action Planning meeting.

"…that is what learning is. You suddenly understand something you've understood all your life, but in a new way."
DORIS LESSING

"Act as though it were impossible to fail."
WINSTON CHURCHILL

"The wise do at once what the fool does later."
BALTASAR GRACIAN (1601-58), SPANISH JESUIT PRIEST AND AUTHOR.

Learning or Idea	Action to be taken	Result Expected

Learning Journal - continued

Learning or Idea	Action to be taken	Result Expected

"Anyone who stops learning is old, whether at twenty or eighty."
HENRY FORD

Learning or Idea	Action to be taken	Result Expected

"*In real life the greatest heroes are often found among the most ordinary people. Do not wait for extraordinary circumstances to do good; try to use ordinary situations.*"

JEAN PAUL RICHTER

Section 3

SKILL DEVELOPMENT ACTION PLAN

Your Skill Development Action Plan is the last Step in the process. After you have completed the Learning Short-take® and all Activities, update your Learning Journal, then complete this section.

SKILL DEVELOPMENT ACTION PLAN

This is the most important part of the program - your individual Skill Development Action Plan.

You need to complete this plan before meeting with your manager or prior to on-going coaching. You will discuss it in detail with your manager or coach as he or she will ensure that you have everything you need to complete the tasks and activities.

Once you have completed your **Skill Development Action Plan** schedule a meeting time with your manager or coach to review your plan. Take your Learning Short-take® and all other documentation received during the training course to this meeting.

Remember - you have committed to your **Skill Development Action Plan**, and need to make time to complete your tasks!

"The mind, once stretched by a new idea, never regains its original dimensions."
OLIVER WENDELL HOLMES

"Whatever you can do or dream you can - begin it. Boldness has genius, power and magic."
JOHANN WOLFGANG VON GOETHE

"Imagination is the eye of the soul."
JOSEPH JOUBERT (1754-1824)

Task or activity (Be specific)	Measure (this will help you to know you have achieved it)	Date (Be specific)
Reflect on your Learning Journal. Transfer action items that you can apply to your job. Ensure that you include some 'stretch goals' and also a blend of short, medium and long term goals.	Apart from you, who else is needed to assist you in achieving your goal.	Be specific. A general date such as 'Quarter 1', 'August', or 'by end of year' is vague and more likely to result in not achieving your target. Be specific – e.g. 22nd November.

IDEAS FOR DISCUSSION WITH MY MANAGER

Ideas

List of DOWNLOADABLE TOOLS

- **Sales Planning Worksheet**
- **Sales Meeting Planner**
- **Sales Meeting Plan Summary**

1. What is the current goal for your business?
2. List up to five sales objectives - what you want to achieve.
3. List the most important things to be done to achieve the results above. (These should be statements of *how* things should be done by the sales force)
4. What components of the product mix are you selling and what is the relative importance of each?
5. What market segments are we going after, and what are their relative priorities?
6. How frequently and on what criteria will my performance and that of my team be measured?
7. Reflect on your draft Sales Goals. Finalize them by rewriting them here.
8. Create a plan of how and to whom will you communicate your sales goals.

CONGRATULATIONS!

You've now completed this Learning Short-take®.

Meet with your Manager/Coach to discuss your
Skill Development Action Plan.

QUICK REFERENCE

This Quick Reference provides you with a summary of key concepts, models and reference material from Learning Short-takes®. We have also included some quotations to ponder.

Use this section as a quick reference to keep your learning active.

Quick Reference

"Actually I'm a good sponge. I absorb ideas and put them to use."

Thomas Alva Edison

Sales Planning

Without a plan there are no definable goals or objectives, no means of evaluating progress, and no ability to measure performance. A Sales Manager's primary function is to collect and evaluate sales data, then develop and execute a plan to achieve team and organizational goals.

Quick Reference

Communication

Through good communication the Sales Manager drives the goals and objectives of the organization. Effective communication means that resources can be managed with less energy, tasks are accomplished with greater speed and accuracy, and there is mutual buy-in at all levels.

SWOT

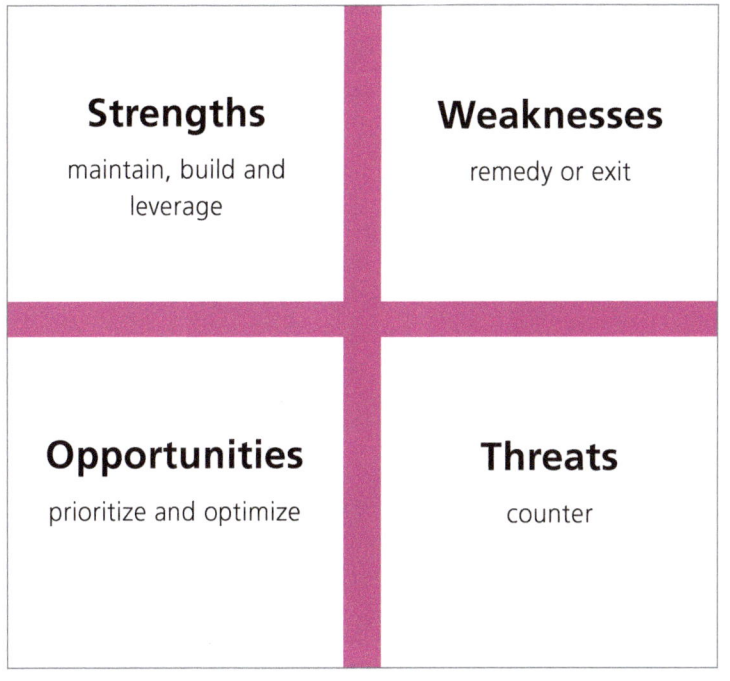

Quick Reference

USP - Unique Selling Proposition (Competitive Advantage)

A concise statement that identifies the unique features that differentiate your products or services from your competitors.

Manage the Sales Team

Distribution Curve of Salespeople

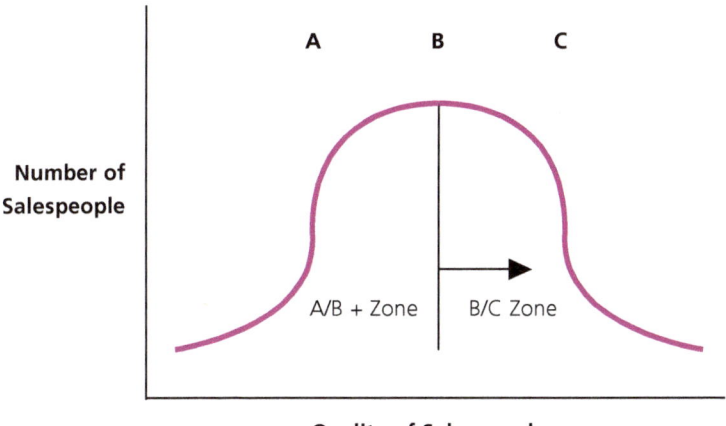

Sales Managers aim to spend 80% of their time with A players, coaching them to become A+ players. Focus on the top performers.

Quick Reference

The Proactive Sales Mix

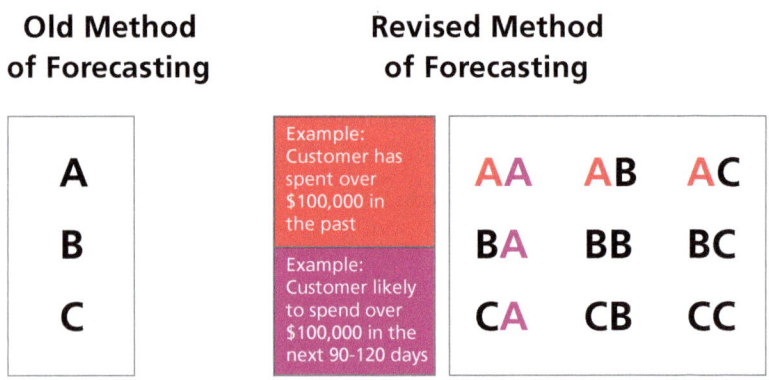

Completed Sales Matrix

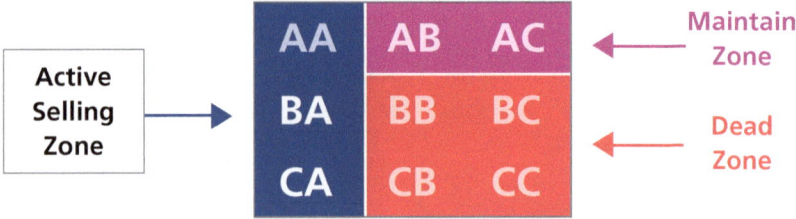

Measuring and Managing Performance

The ability to accurately predict changes in revenue, margins, expenses, competitive actions, market needs and wants, and the potential of the sales team is key to sales success.

Quick Reference

> **The best executive is the one who has sense enough to pick good men to do what he wants done, and self-restraint enough to keep from meddling with them while they do it.**
>
> — Theodore Roosevelt

Sales Measures

Be specific about what you want your salespeople to do. Sample frequency metrics include:

- Sales calls per week
- Weekly prospecting
- Home office visits
- Reports on time

- Sales proposals per week
- Executive sales calls
- Sales funnel quantity
- Sales calls on key accounts

- Executive visits
- Demonstrations
- Focus on A prospects
- Time Management

Great Sales People

Hiring the best salespeople is critical to the performance of the sales team. When recruiting great salespeople they should:

- Have a natural curiosity
- Take 'complex' and make it 'simple'
- Have the ability to 'flip'
- See things from all perspectives

> **Leaders don't create followers, they create more leaders.**
>
> Tom Peters

Quick Reference

Active Selling Time

3 hours per day for what?

Deploying the Sales Team

Types of Sales Territories

Type of Sales Territory	Advantages	Disadvantages
Geographic	<ul><li>Easy, Clean, and Minimal Disputes</li><li>Less Travel Cost</li><li>Deeper Geographical Penetration</li></ul>	<ul><li>Less Specialization</li><li>Less Customer Continuity</li><li>Constant Change with Growth</li></ul>
Account	<ul><li>High Customer Centric</li><li>Deep Industry Penetration</li><li>High in Relationship Selling</li><li>Maximizes 80/20 Rule</li></ul>	<ul><li>Higher Travel Budgets</li><li>Less Geographic Coverage</li><li>Low New Account Focus</li></ul>
Product	<ul><li>High Value-Add Sale Approach</li><li>Adaptable to Fast-Changing Products</li><li>Market Penetration</li></ul>	<ul><li>Less Relationship Selling</li><li>Less Customer Focus</li><li>Can Get Complex</li></ul>

Quick Reference

Making Sales Meetings Work

Reactive Sales Meeting Focus	Proactive Sales Meeting Focus
1. Product knowledge 2. Company speakers 3. Team building 4. Free time 5. Communication skills	1. Selling skills 2. Communication/ presentation skills 3. Product knowledge 4. Teambuilding 5. Company speakers

> **A good leader is a person who takes a little more than his share of the blame and a little less than his share of the credit.**
>
> John C Maxwell

"

"Leadership can be thought of as a capacity to define oneself to others in a way that clarifies and expands a vision of the future."

EDWIN H. FRIEDMAN

NEXT STEPS

Congratulations! You have now completed this Learning Short-take® title. The entire list of Learning Short-takes® can be found on the catherinemattiske.com website.

In this section we have suggested Learning Short-take® titles for you that will build your learning. You may order these Learning Short-takes® online at https://www.catherinemattiske.com/books or from your bookstores.

Influencing for Opportunity
Identify and Maximize Ways to Influence

Course Content

- Part 1: Fundamentals of Influence
- Part 2: Influence: A Choice
- Part 3: Naturally Occurring Influence Patterns
- Part 4: Methods of Persuasion
- Part 5: The Challenges of Influence
- Part 6: Building a life of Influence

Learning Short-take® Outline

Influencing for Opportunity combines self-study with realistic workplace activities to provide you with the key skills and techniques to influence those around you. You will learn the theory of influence, influence principles and strategies, as well as how to plan and prepare for important opportunities to influence. As a result, you should achieve greater results in your organization, work more productively and effectively in a team environment, and develop stronger working relationships with co-workers, suppliers and customers.

The ability to influence others is critical in today's competitive business environment. Being highly skilled in influence enables you to build the relationships you need to get results inside or outside the organization. Employees and managers alike cannot assume they have power over others - they must earn it through influence. Being an influential person is a skill that can be learned and practiced. **Influencing for Opportunity** will help you succeed in the modern corporate environment by increasing your ability to influence others.

Influencing for Opportunity includes a **toolkit of job aids and learning support tools** provided to you as free downloads.

Learning Objectives

- Identify patterns of influence.
- Evaluate how you currently use influence behaviors and identify areas for development.
- Develop influence behaviors for greater personal and business success.
- Establish clear and powerful influence goals.
- Increase influence to overcome resistance.
- Describe how to ask for and receive support.
- Design an approach for formal and informal influence situations; apply the approach to a real-life situation.
- Create a Skill Development Action Plan.

Persuasive Presentation Skills
Create, Prepare and Design with Confidence

Learning Short-take® Outline
Persuasive Presentation Skills combines self-study with realistic workplace activities to provide presenters with the key skills and techniques to prepare and deliver dynamic presentations. After assessing your current approach to preparing and delivering presentations, **Persuasive Presentation Skills** will help you develop unique and innovative strategies to improve your presentation success from small meetings to large audiences. You will learn to effectively plan your communication by using a real-life upcoming presentation.

A dynamic and powerful presentation gives you a platform to communicate your message effectively, influence your audience and spark desired action. Effective presenters spend a considerable amount of time preparing for their presentation, ensuring that the structure, content and communication style is appropriate for their audience. It is often what happens before the presenter gives their presentation that dictates the success of the presentation.

Persuasive Presentation Skills includes the **Persuasive Presentation Skills Presentation Planner**, provided as a free downloadable tool.

Learning Objectives
- Define the importance of preparation in delivering a successful presentation.
- Know how to structure your presentation to deliver key messages.
- Recognize how to connect with your audience and maintain attention.
- Identify key factors for enhancing your message and projecting credibility.
- Design and use visual aids to support your message.
- Describe how to control your nervous energy.
- Create a Skill Development Action Plan.

Course Content
- Part 1: Creating Effective Presentations
  - Overview for Success
- Part 2: Planning Your Presentation
  - 7 Steps for Success
- Part 3: The Presentation Day
  - Reducing Nervousness
  - Tips & Tricks
  - After the Presentation

In Closing…

The Effective Leader
Skills and Tools for Inspired Leadership

Learning Short-take® Outline

The Effective Leader will guide managers and leaders at all levels towards maximizing your effectiveness as a leader in the workplace. By demystifying the key concepts of communication, team building, leadership styles, individual and team motivation, performance, and interpersonal skills, you will be better equipped for success in your leadership role.

The Effective Leader includes covers both the essential theory and practical skills for successful leadership of teams. Through a series of self-assessment and action learning activities you will identify the differences between management and leadership, write a vision and mission statements, and identify your natural leadership style.
The Effective Leader will illustrate how to use additional leadership styles and how to plan and lead effective team meetings.

Increased leadership skills moves individuals and teams to increased resilience in the face of change, enhanced performance and greater success!

The Effective Leader includes the **Meeting Planner, Meeting Agenda, Core Essentials of Compelling Vision & Mission Statements Job Aid,** and the **Leadership Styles Summary,** provided as free downloadable tools.

Learning Objectives

- Define the relationship between leadership and management.
- Understand the meaning of vision, mission and values.
- Know the role of leader as coach.
- Apply the theory of the functional and situational approaches to leadership.
- Work on the personal qualities of leadership and display the will to lead.
- Have a high regard for communication in the leadership process and develop the ability to communicate.
- List ways to influence motivation for each member of your team.
- Create a Skill Development Action Plan

Course Content

- Part 1: The Effective Leader
- Part 2: Management vs Leadership
- Part 3: Leadership Vision & Mission
- Part 4: Leadership Styles
- Part 5: Understanding Behavior
- Part 6: Leadership & Roles
- Part 7: Leading a Team

www.catherinemattiske.com

www.ingramcontent.com/pod-product-compliance
Lightning Source LLC
Chambersburg PA
CBHW042230090526
44587CB00001B/13